BEST OF
BAR DESIGN

drink!

Imprint
The Deutsche Bibliothek is registering this publication in the Deutsche Nationalbibliographie detailed bibliographical information can be found on the internet at http://dnb.ddb.de

ISBN 978-3-03768-015-5
© 2009 by Braun Publishing AG
www.braun-publishing.ch

1st edition 2009

Project coordinator: Annika Schulz
Editorial staff: Dagmar Glück
Translation: Stephen Roche, Hamburg
Graphic concept: Michaela Prinz

BEST OF
BAR DESIGN

BRAUN

drink!

Preface

The bar is essential to the mythology of the city. We plunge into it, quaff an expertly mixed Manhattan, and experience an immediate sense of well-being. What is it that produces this unique atmosphere? The bartender and his cocktails, of course; the people and the music. But all of that would be nothing without the designed space, and its particular lighting, forms and materials. The bar appeals to all of the senses; it is the architectural embodiment of the night. But even though one can get a Manhattan in any bar, no two bars are the same. Bars are a rewarding playground for architects and designers. This is where they live out their most creative ideas, experimenting with unusual materials, colors and innovative techniques. They take up the challenge to create durable and lasting interior spaces in unconventional yet also trend-setting designs. The design of a bar is based on the ideas of the owner and the profile of the target customers. The borders between a nightclub, restaurant and café are often fluid; thus an interior that appears purely functional by day can be immersed in dim light in the evening, revealing a cool lounge. Drink! Best of Bar Design presents a wide variety of contemporary interior design, ranging from the classic hotel bar to a beach bar with a harmonious design idiom that melts into the Portuguese sun. Juxtaposed with these is a contemporary interpretation of the traditional wine cellar, which sparkles with a novel brilliance thanks to an abundance of glass and an open design plan.

While bars come in many shapes and sizes, they have a common heart – the bar counter. That is, after all, what gives

the bar its name. It has its origins in the Wild West. Firewater was first served in small drugstores. Many a boozy night ended in a wild brawl, so the storeowners erected a 'barrier' in front of the shelves to protect both themselves and their liquor. Thus the word bar entered our language. Gradually these primitive taprooms evolved into the more refined saloons, and the 'American bar' was born. In Europe of the same era customers were still served at tables, but with the increase in international travel soon the first bar counters began to appear in high-class hotels.

The age of the cowboys is long gone, and the bars of today must satisfy a style-conscious and very mixed clientele. Whether hip party people, smart society ladies, adventure-seeking tourists or respectable businesspeople, some bars seek a specific clientele while others derive their flair precisely through achieving a successful mix. Design plays a key role in determining the character of a bar. Thus, for example, the Conte is famous for having the longest bar counter in the city (Alexander Brenner Architect). In the classically designed Bar N in Nagoya, Japan the bar counter is built from the wood of a single cedar tree (Hiroyuki Miyake Design Office). Back-lit bottles on a wall constructed from Ooya stone provide the main light source. In addition to the furnishings, the choice of building materials plays a decisive role in creating a bar's mood and image. The FEEK BAR (FEEK) in Antwerp, for example, creates a playful image by using off-beat marshmallow furniture. By contrast, London's Bordello Bar (Sam Buxton) has a deliberately disreputable feel. Miles of woolen yarn have been used to give the walls the appearance of mesh pantyhose. Yet whatever the love of quirky detail, every bar must meet certain practical requirements: the bar counter must work even when the bar is packed, all ingredients and glasses must be within the bartender's reach, and all materials must be easy to clean.

The customer remains blissfully unaware of the organizational aspects of tending bar. He contentedly sips his Singapore Sling and allows his gaze to wander. The lighting in a bar influences the mood. Alongside materials and furnishings it is a decisive and much utilized design element. In the Revolution Lounge in Las Vegas, for example, the lighting installations evoke the Sixties. By contrast, the restrained lighting design of DCB in Tokyo (Love the Life) creates a mystical feeling. This classic bar is the perfect metaphor of a moonlit night.

Lighting and materials, form and music, people from various social strata – when all of these factors come together in the right mixture then the bar itself becomes the perfect cocktail. It is an enchanting parallel world, created purely to celebrate the night. Let's raise one last glass to that.

The **base is milled** from uncut polyethylene **pipe** and **weldes** to the seat

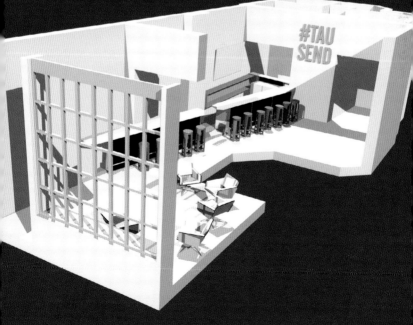

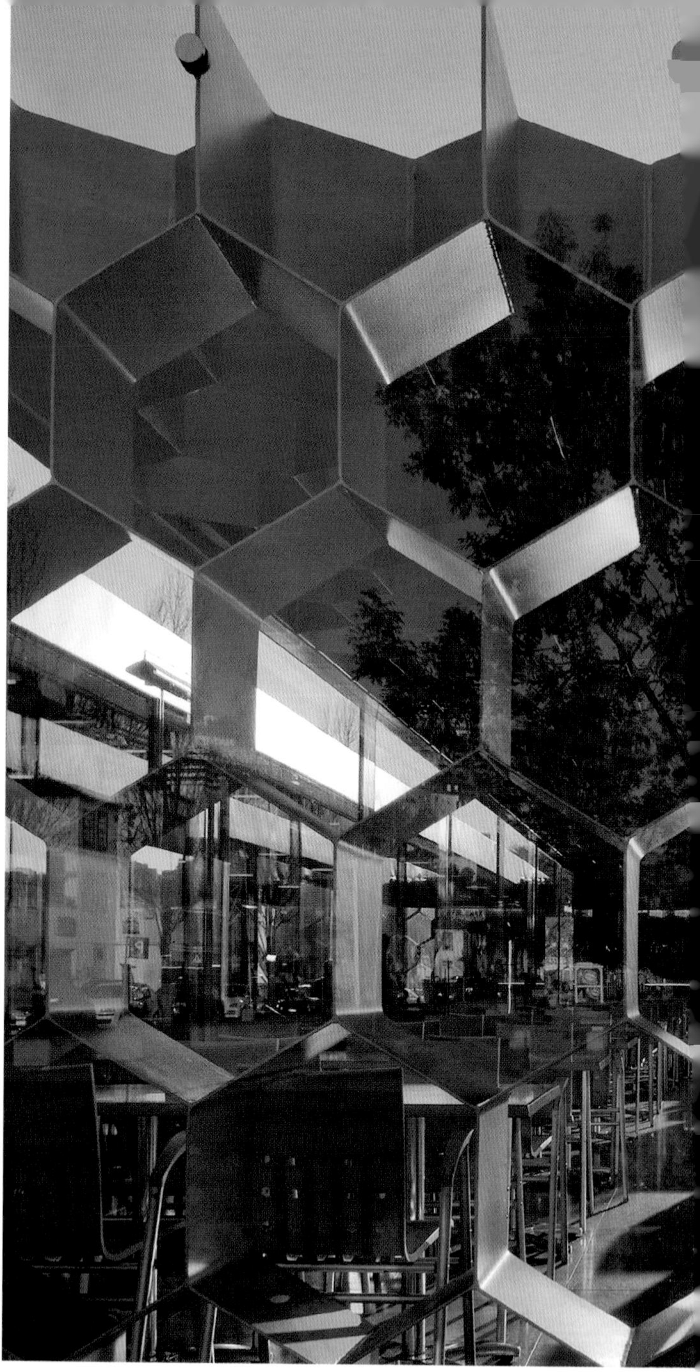

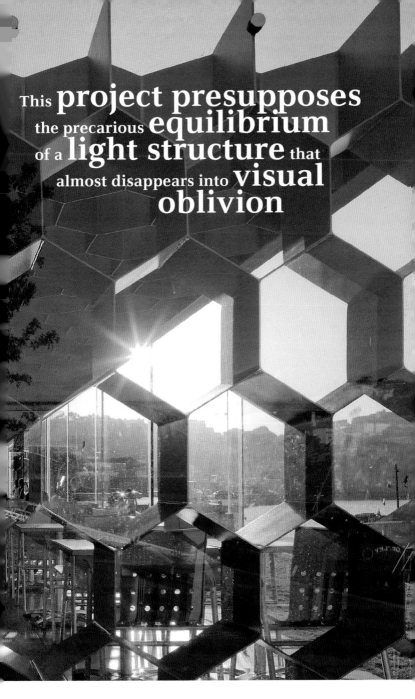

This **project presupposes** the precarious **equilibrium** of a **light structure** that almost disappears into **visual oblivion**

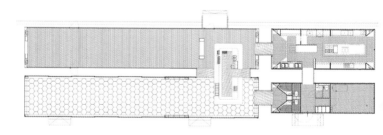

A **mixture** of **compute technology** and **traditional** building techniqu

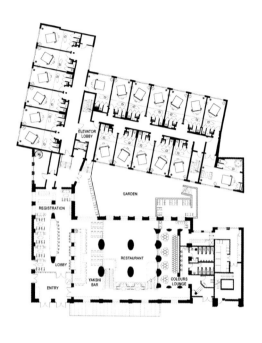

ELEVATOR
LOBBY

GARDEN

REGISTRATION

RESTAURANT

LOBBY

YAKSHI
BAR

COLOURS
LOUNGE

ENTRY

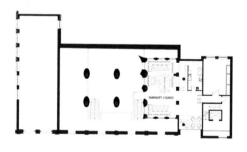

SMIRNOFF LOUNGE

Classic materials are placed in a new context thank to a novel use of color an spatial design

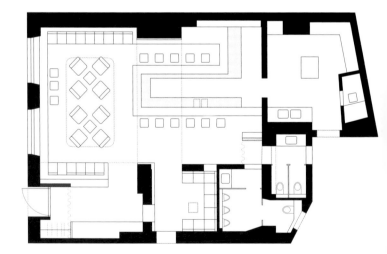

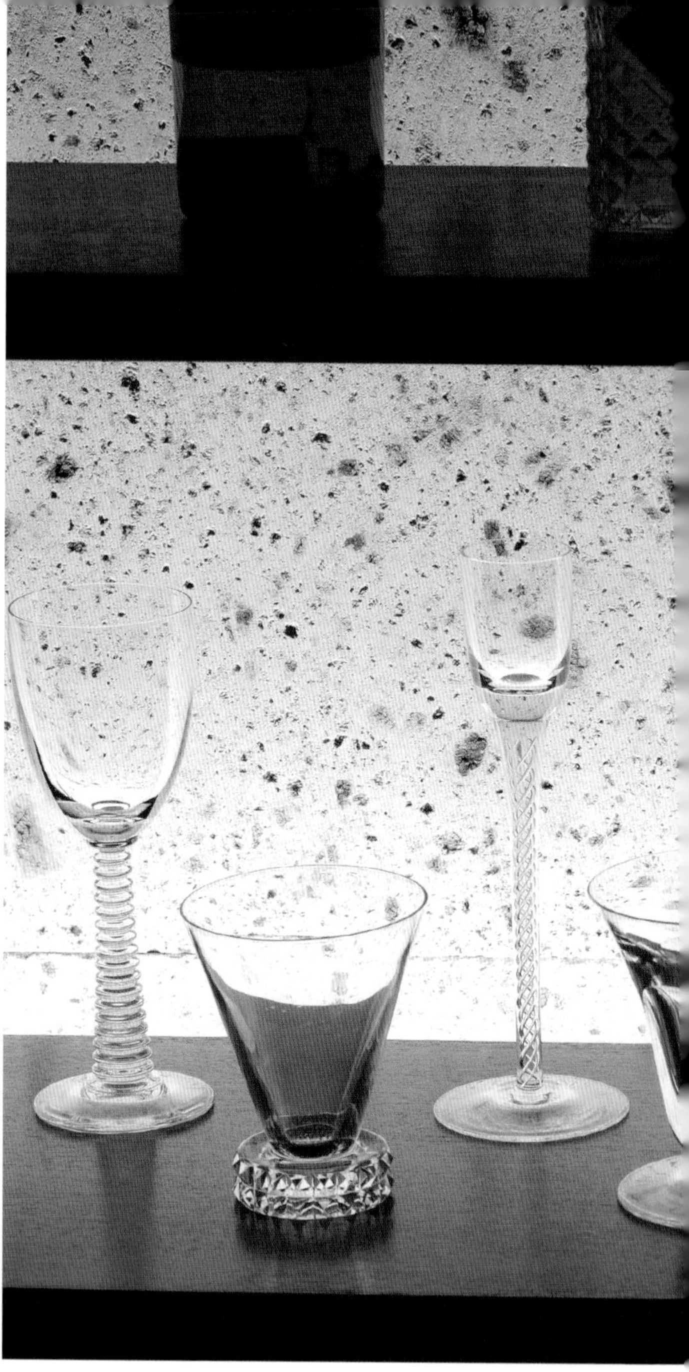

The **counter** is **carved** from a **single** Japanese **cedar**

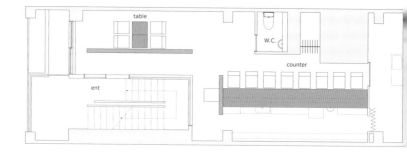

481 **Barlounge 808** | Berlin | plajer & franz studio

Distinctive elements such as an aquarium, alcoves and customized furniture create a relaxed atmosphere

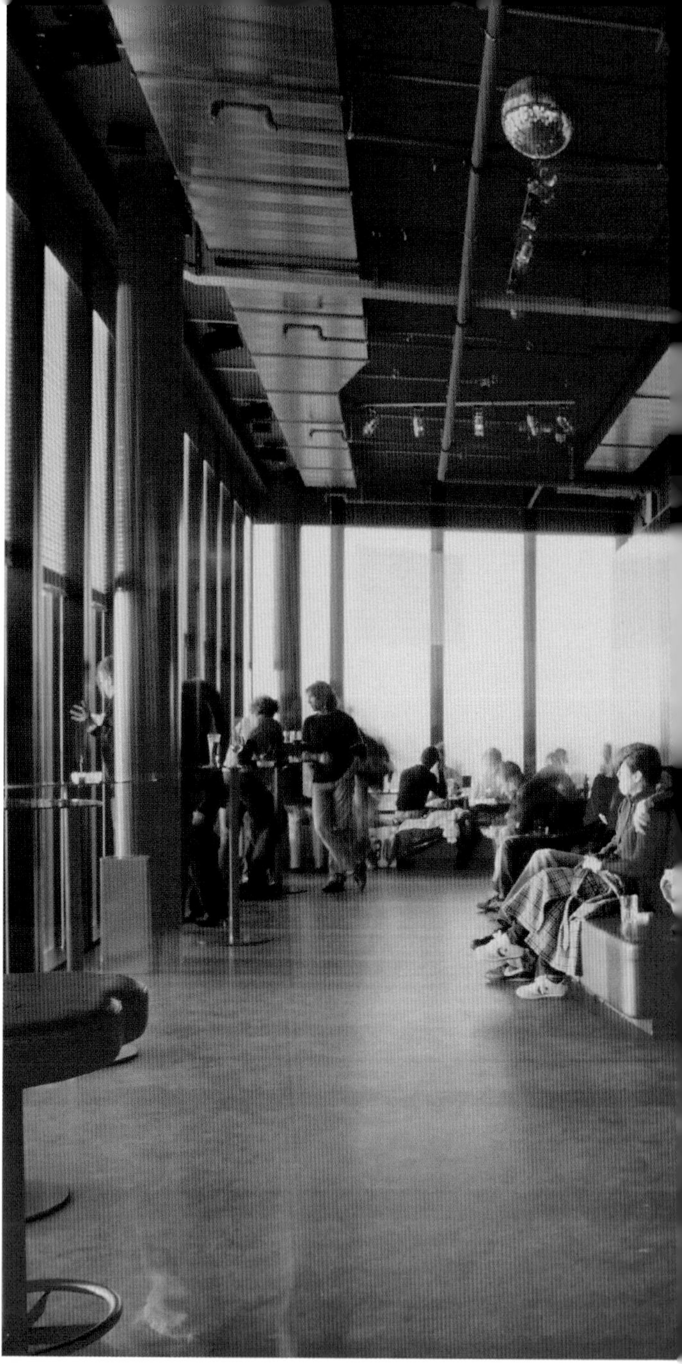

A **world** of **stimulation**
for **all the senses**

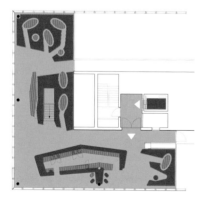

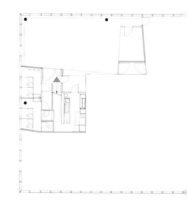

This is a **contemporary interpretation** of a traditional **wine cellar**

beaudevin®

ALL THE BEAUTY OF WINE

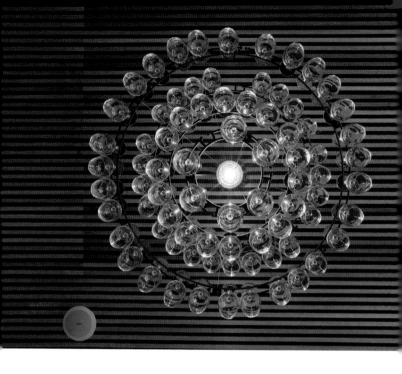

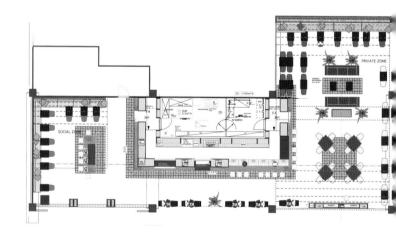

The **smooth, clean line**
of the furniture and interior **mat**
the **gentle curves** of the buil

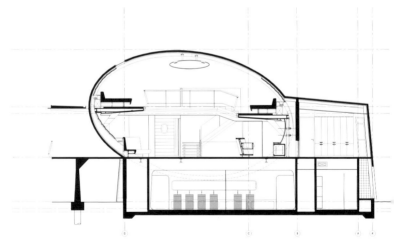

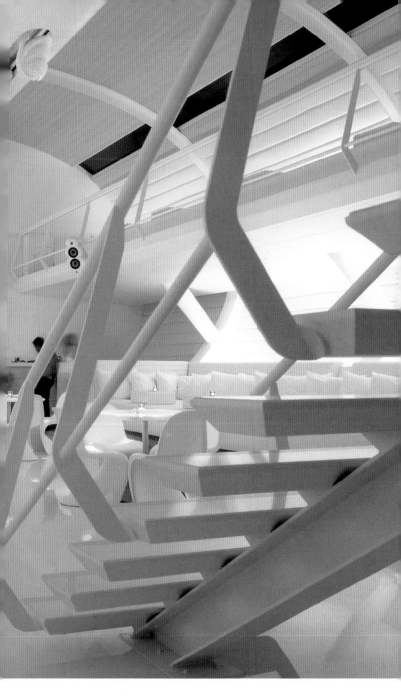

BMW Museum, M1 Café Bar | Munich | ATELIER BRÜCKNER

Corian and **BMW leather** are the **defining features** of this light, **white space**

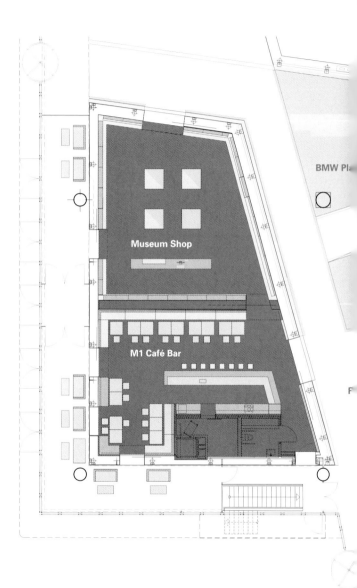

BMW Pl

Museum Shop

M1 Café Bar

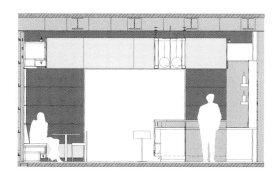

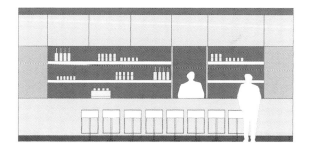

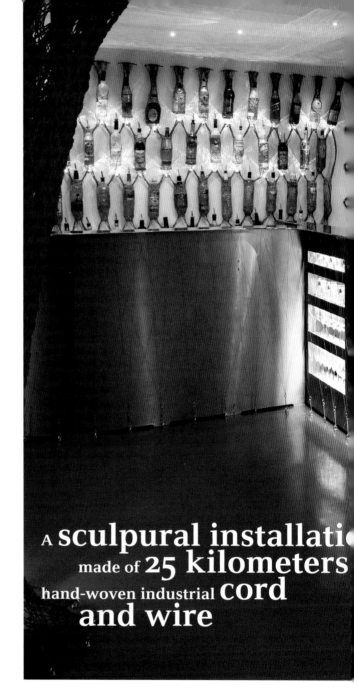

A **sculpural installati**
made of **25 kilometers**
hand-woven industrial **cord**
and wire

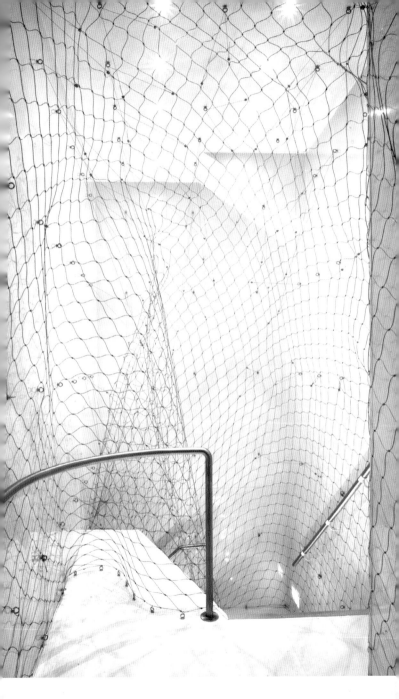

104 | **Café Ceol** | Bangor | John Robb Interiors

A cocktail bar with a contemporary nod to the Parisian salon

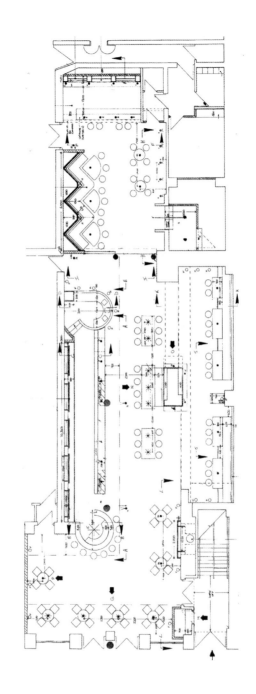

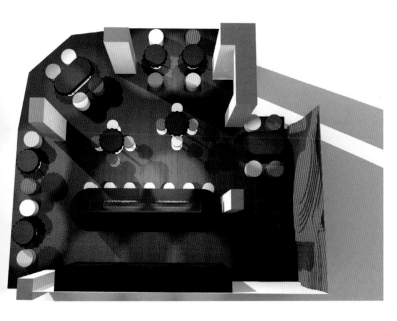

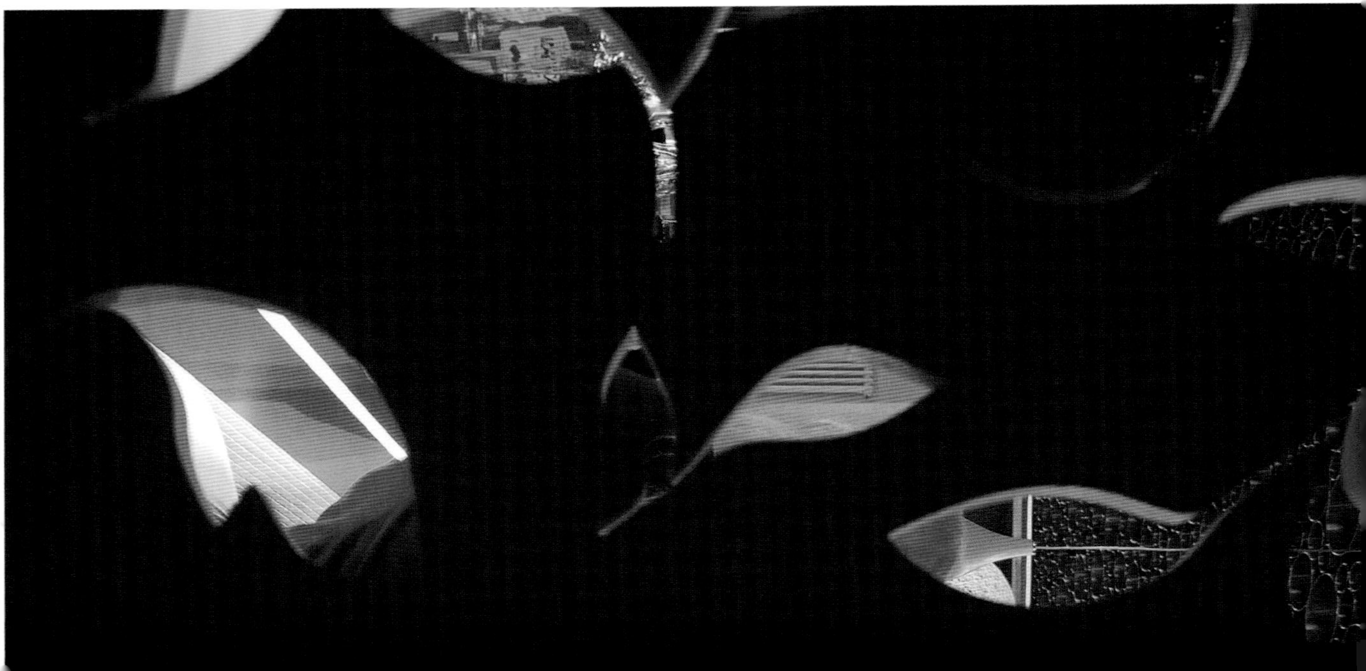

The café as fashionable meeting place

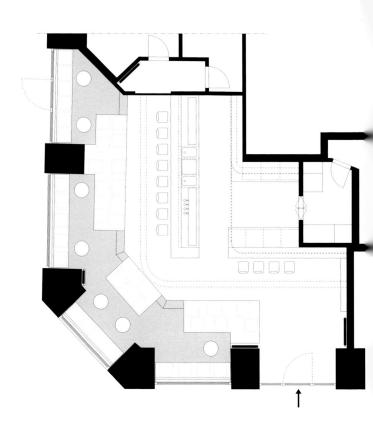

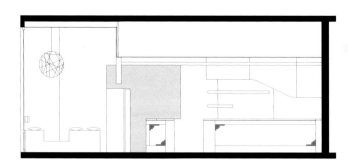

Centrale I Stuttgart I Alexander Brenner Architect

A **small room** for
life's **little celebrations**

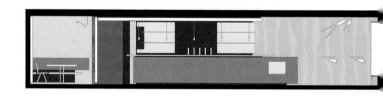

126 | **The Clinic at Clarke Quay** | Singapore | Concrete Architectural Associates

The floor plan is **composed** of **different modules,** each offering its **own form,** ambiance and **experience**

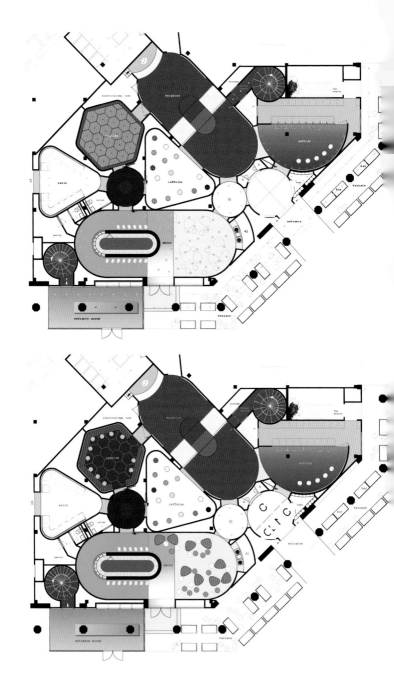

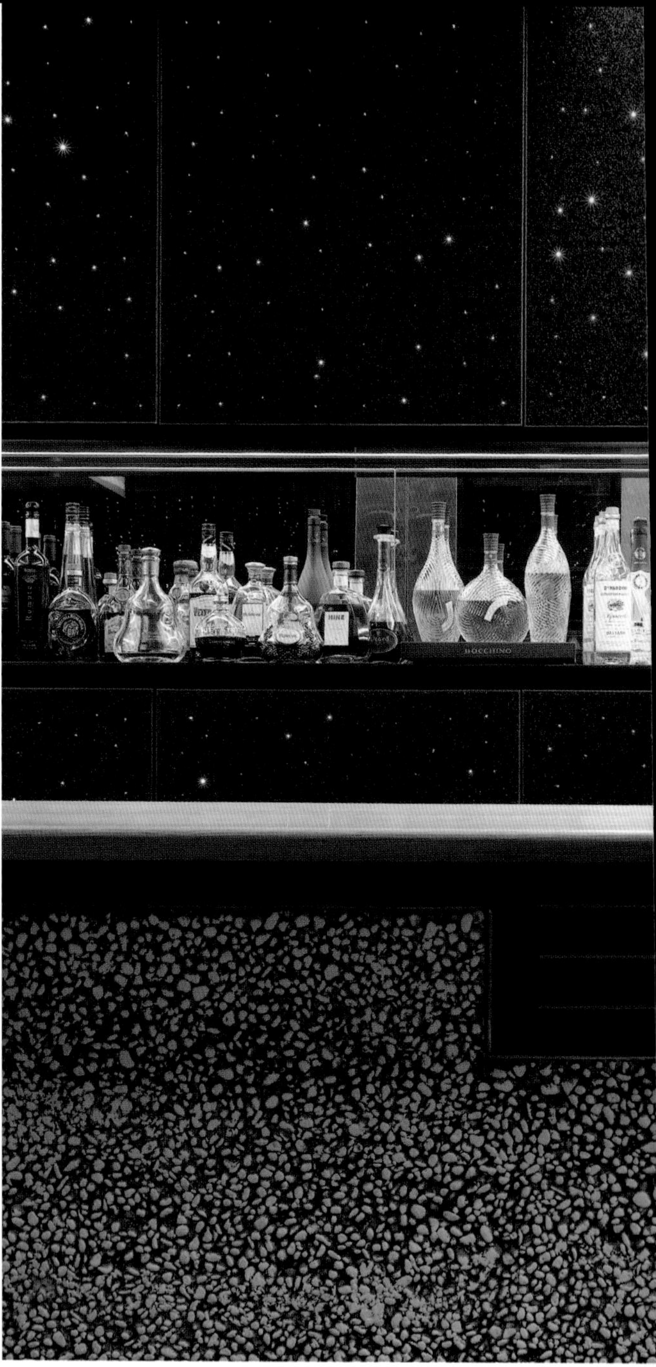
BOCCHINO

Famous for
the **longest bar** in town

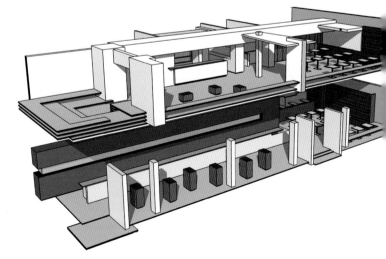

148 | **Dahlberg Gastropub** | Helsingborg | Mental Design

An experience for
all the senses

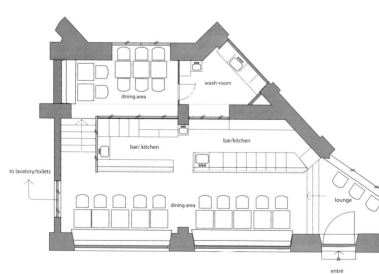

wash-room

dining area

bar/ kitchen

bar/kitchen

to lavatory/toilets

dining area

lounge

entré

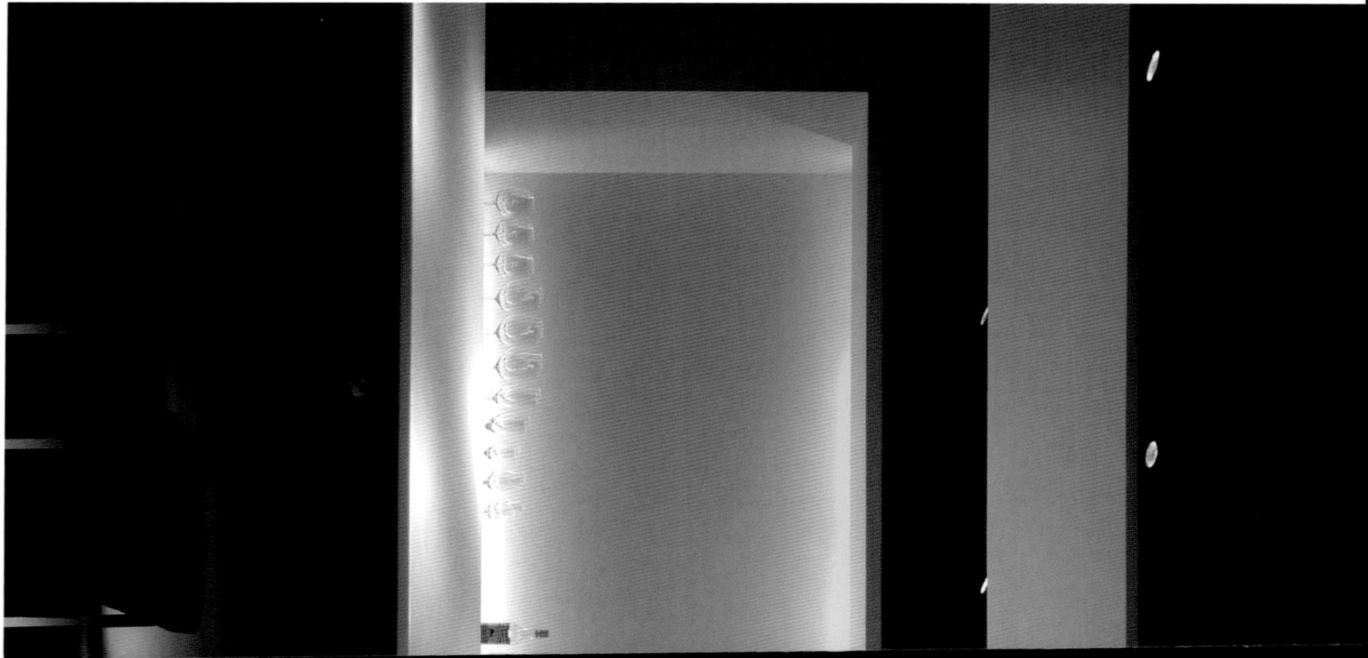

This **design** is a **metaphor** for a moonlit **night**

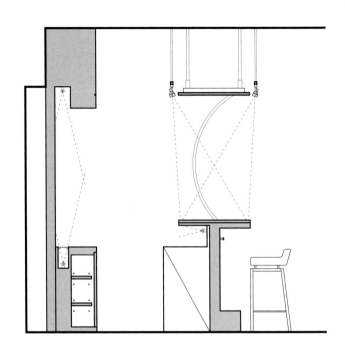

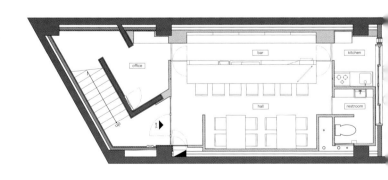

164 | **Downtown Bar** | Milwaukee | Johnsen Schmaling Architects

The ribbon's **deep red color** washes the **entire space** with a sensuous **incandescence**

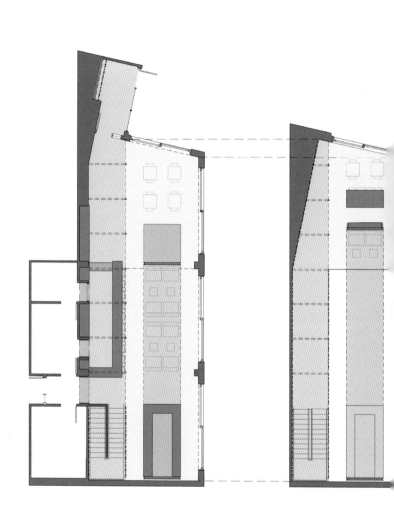

174 | **Escape Bar** | São Paulo | Arthur Casas Arquiteture e Design

The idea was to **create a** kind of **urban refuge**

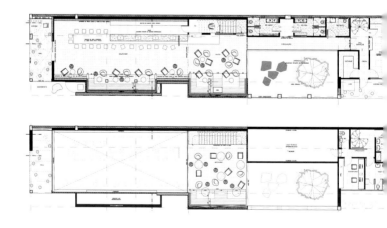

186 | **FEEK BAR** | Antwerp | FEEK

The latest in **coated materials,** a design concept **involving soft** acoustic walls and **'marshmallow' furniture**

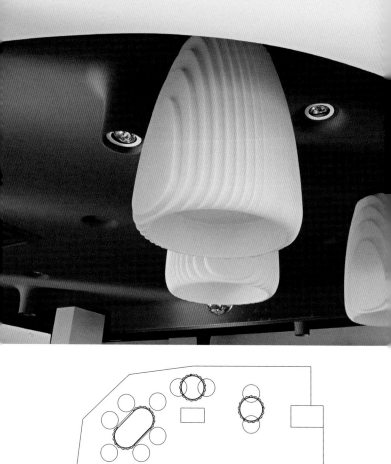

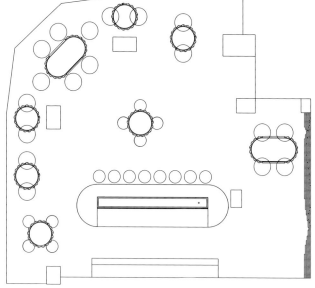

194 | **frame bar** | Athens | DImitrios Tsigos / TDC

Using forms that morph from one geometry to another, thus defying definition

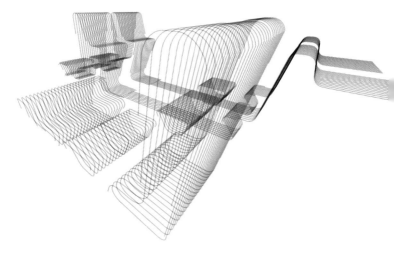

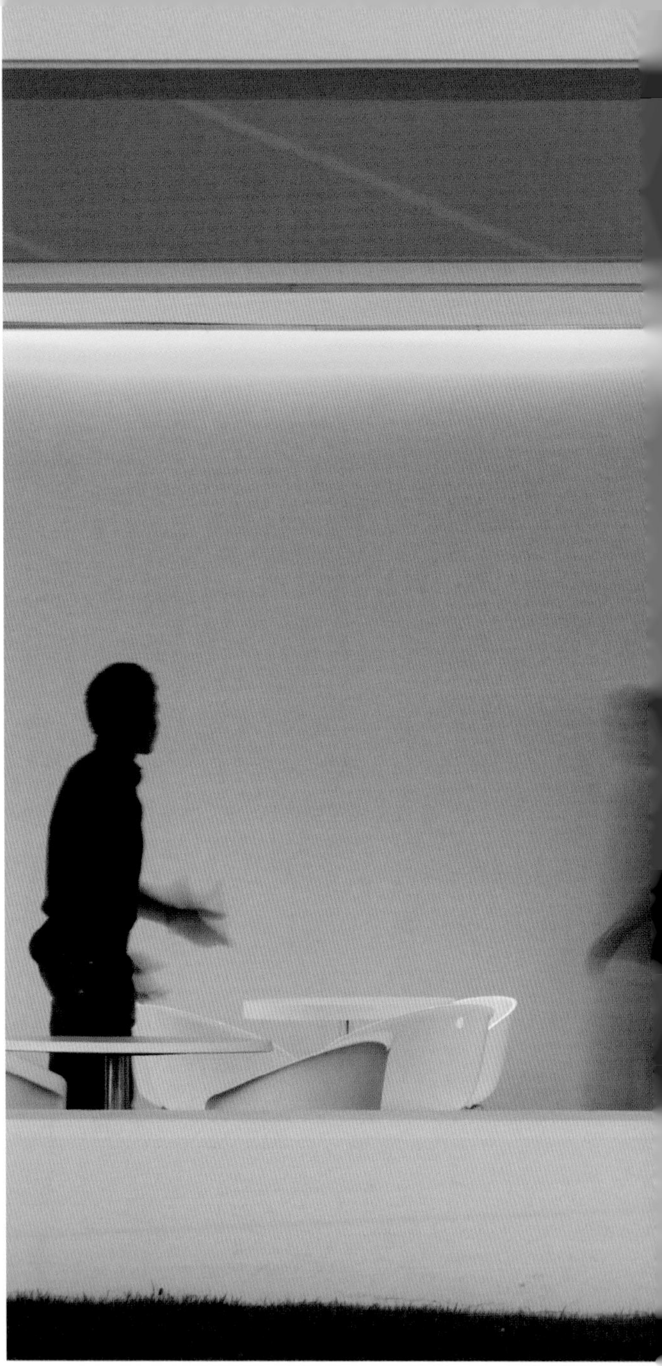

Functional integrity, plasticity, light and color are combined seamlessly

212 | **Hotel Drei Raben – Die Lounge** | Nuremberg | Claus Lämmle Bueroplasz

Defined by the **interplay of light,** form, **material** and **space**

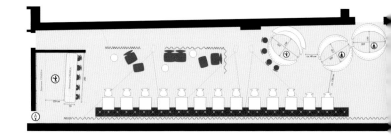

An **impulsive composition** of mod materials and **historical details**

Klubb Rouge | Beijing | Andromeda International

A **sophisticated blend** of **Chinese tradition** and the **new spirit** of the city

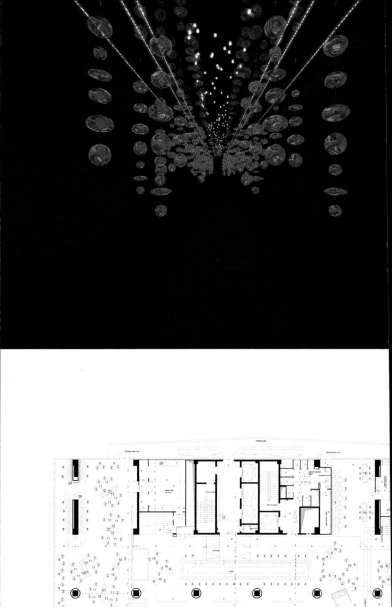

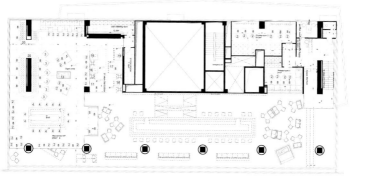

Lounge Bar 5 Sentidos | Girona | ON-A Jordi Fernández / Eduardo Gutiérrez

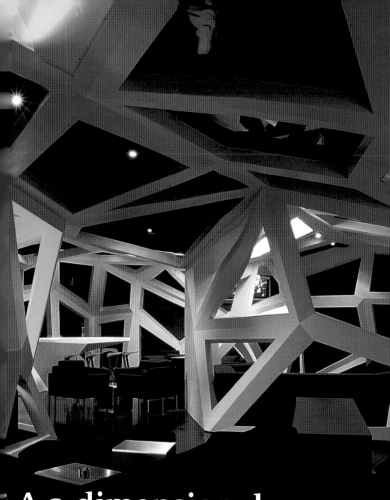

A 3-dimensional
net, irregular, deformed,
stretched and moulded

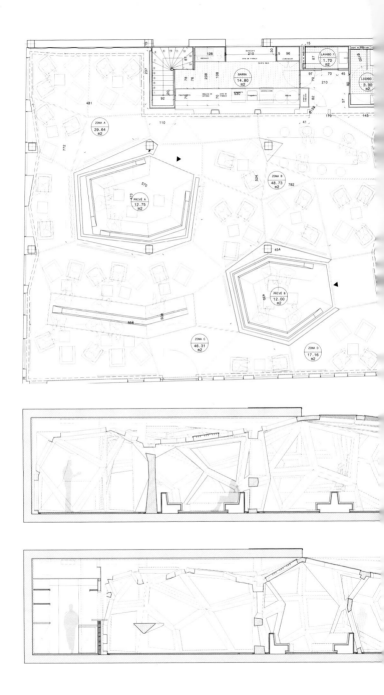

This interior **exudes** captivating **elegance** and a **relaxe** atmosphere

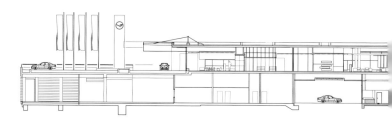

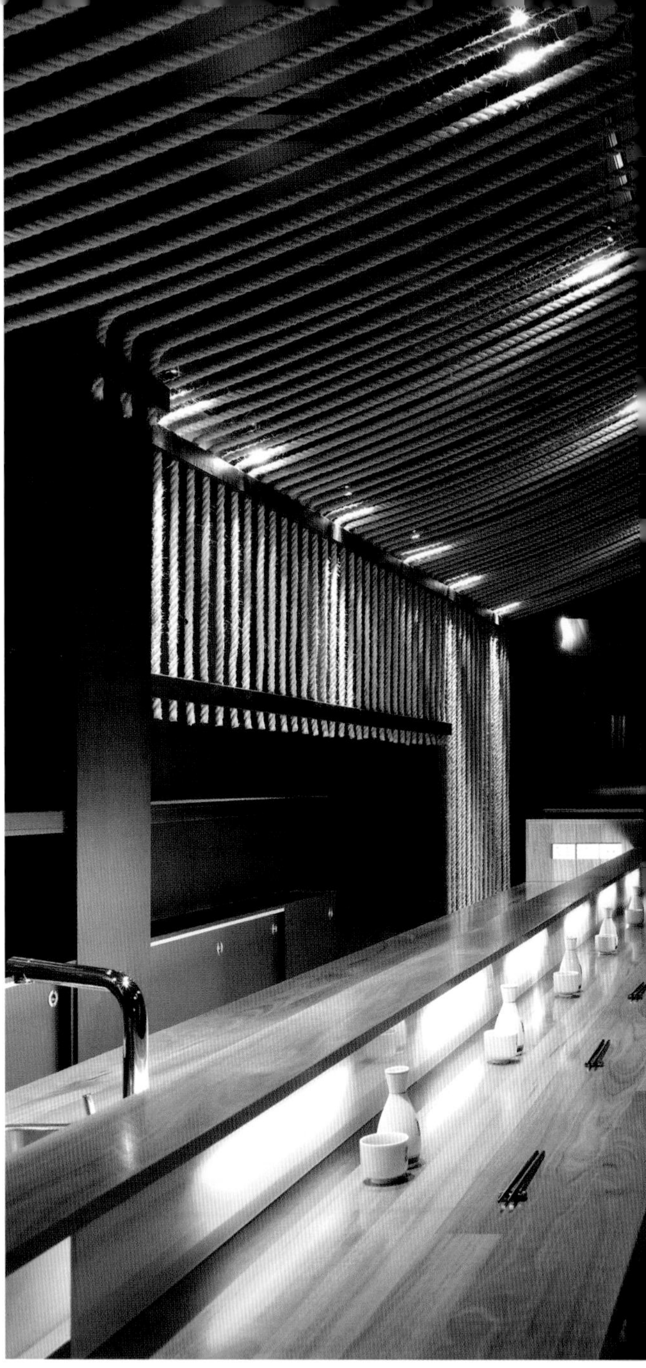

The **principle materials** used here are **Manila ropes,** timber and **concrete**

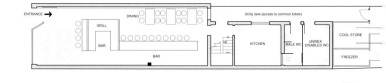

ENTRANCE →

DINING

GRILL

BAR

BAR

Utility lane (access to common toilets)

UP

KITCHEN

MALE WC

UNISEX DISABLED WC

COOL STORE

FREEZER

Majik Café | Belgrade | Karim Rashid Inc.

The dynamic patterned glass bar changes color and mood throughout the customer's stay

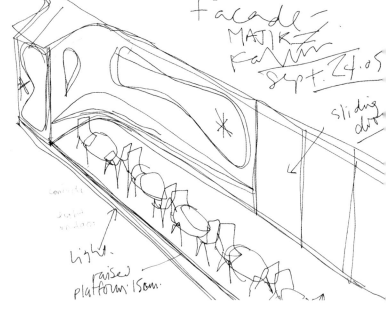

facade—
MAJIK
KAFIM
Sept. 24.05

sliding
do[?]

contract[?]
[?]
light.
raised
platform. 15cm.

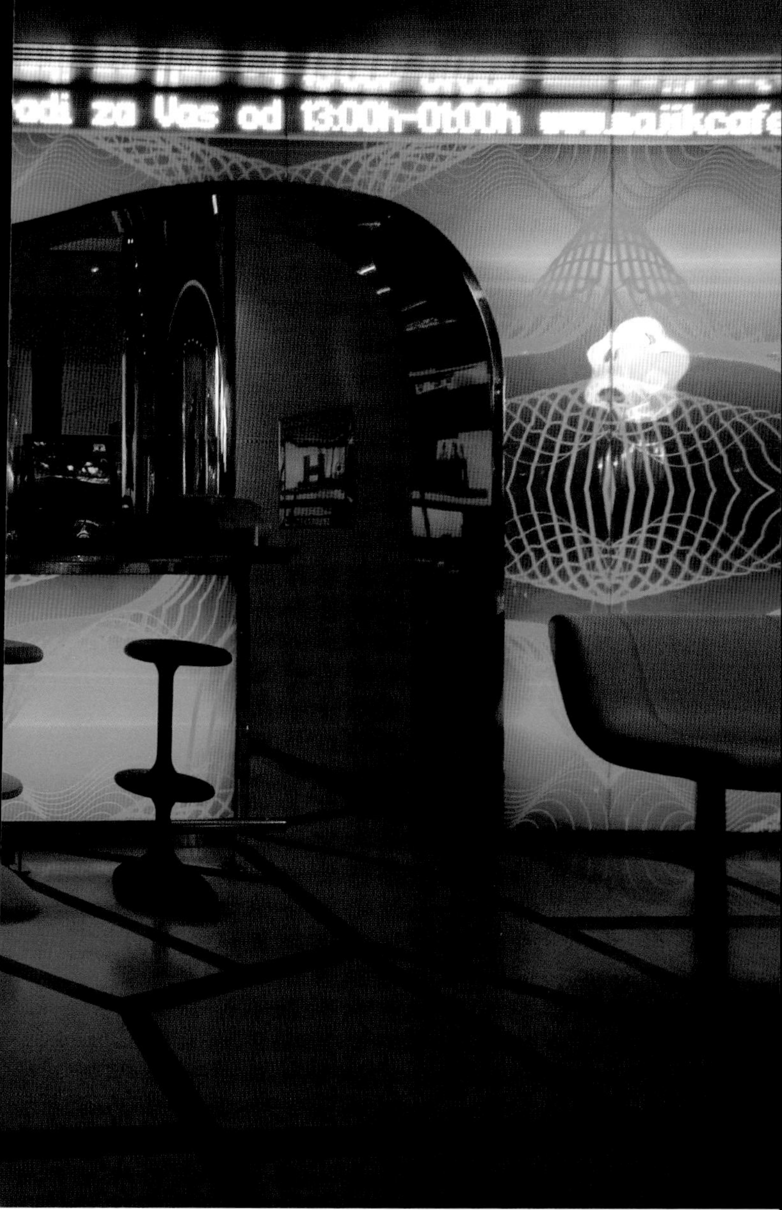
za Vas od 13:00h-01:00h

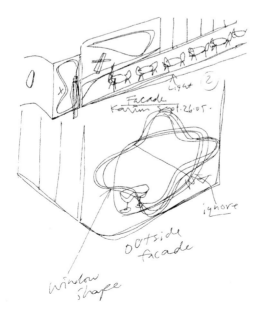

Facade
Karim Sept. 26. 05.

Light 2

ignore

Outside
facade

window
shape

276 | **Oulu Bar & EcoLounge** | Brooklyn | Evangeline Dennie, LEED AP / / / Design / Architecture / Sustainability

High performing
eco-friendly materials **were**
incorporated throughout
the **design**

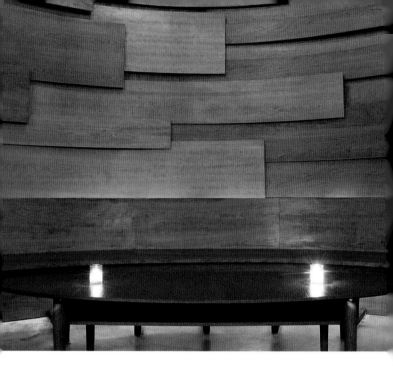

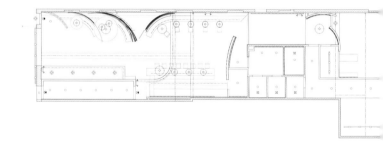

Creating an entertainment space for adults

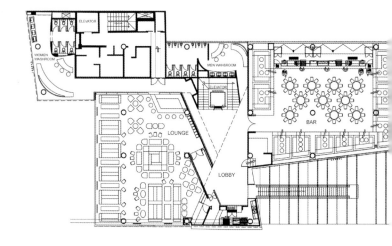

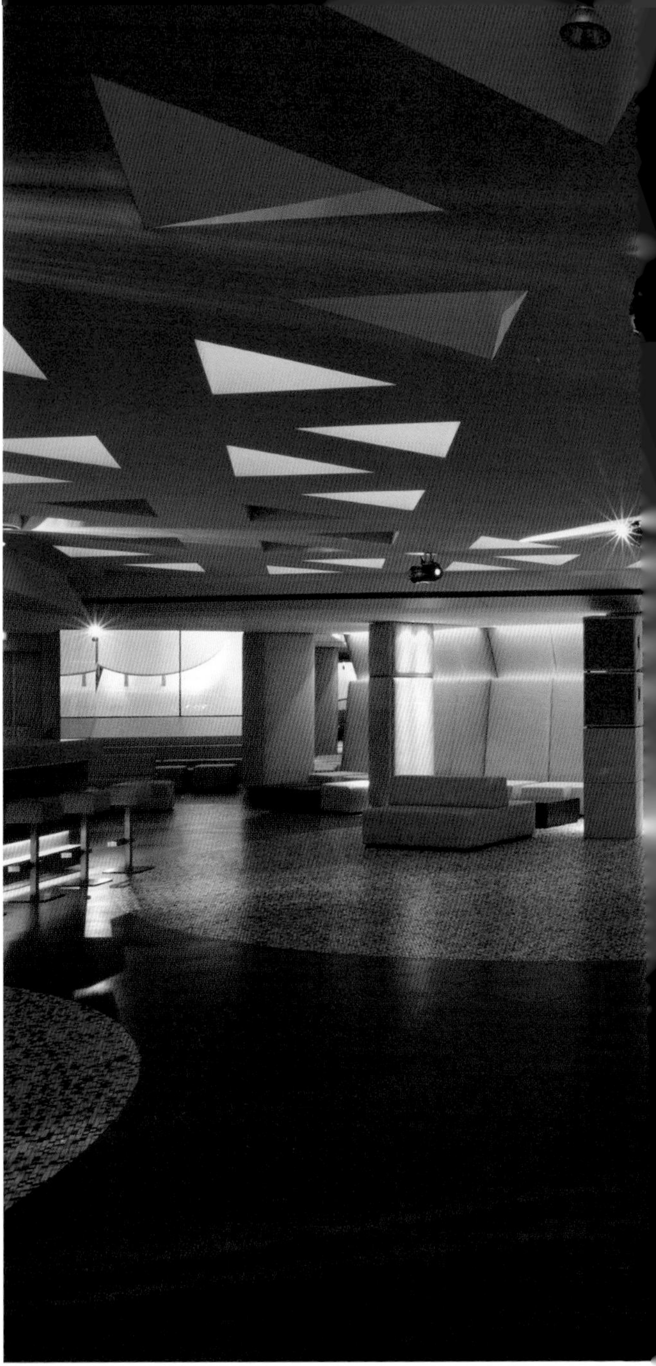

The **lighting design** creates a **variety of interesting** atmospheres

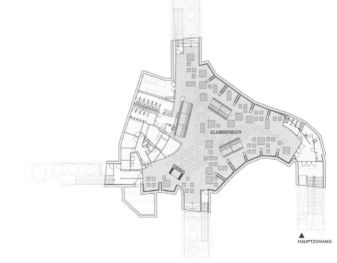

CLUBBEREICH

HAUPTZUGANG

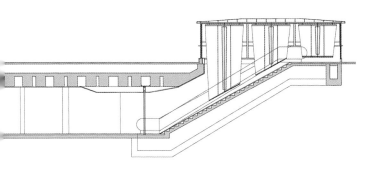

Peacock Dinner Club | Stockholm | OLSSONLYCKEFORS ARCHITECTS

Different materials, lighting effects and pattern allow various spaces to dissolve into one anothe

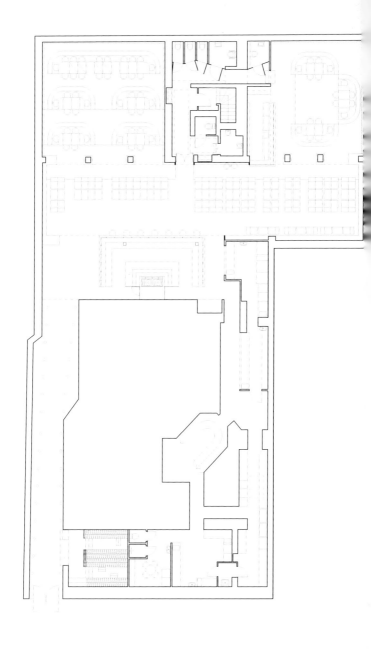

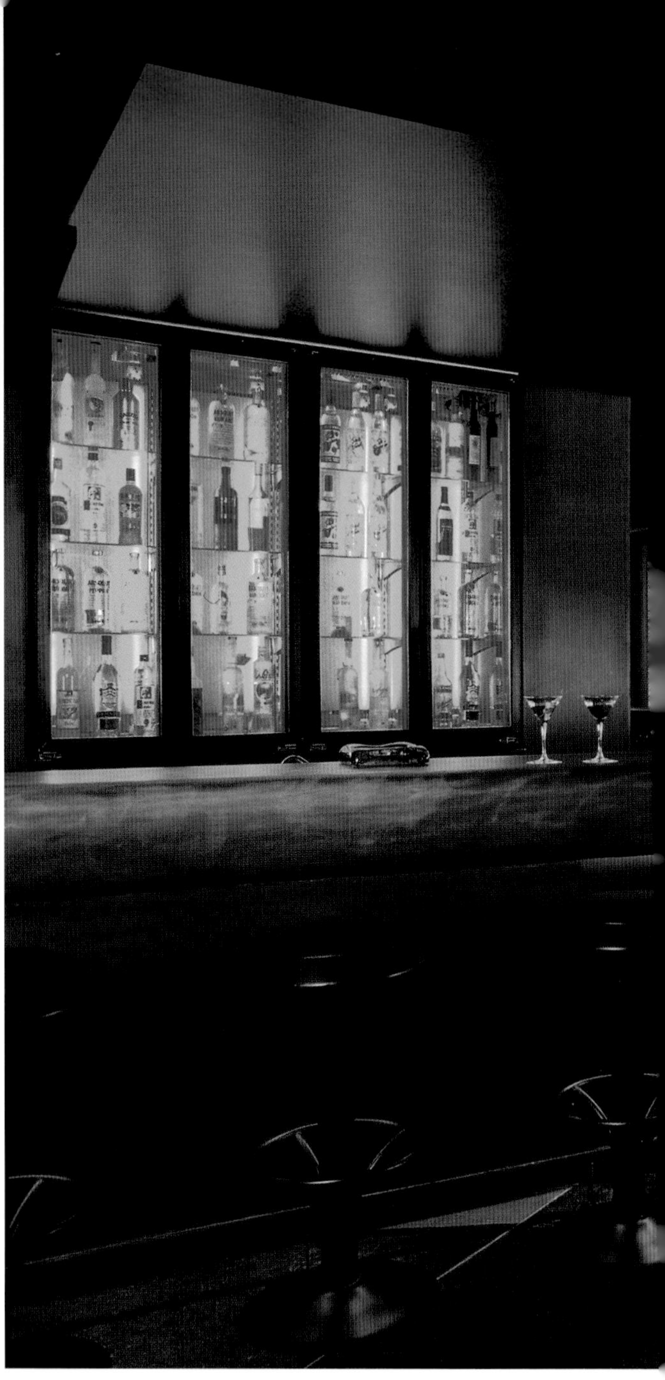

A traditional **Thai house** is transformed into a **stylish bar**

Revolution Lounge | Las Vegas | CIRQUE DU SOLEIL, Humà, MF

Installations that evoke the **Sixties** while re-telling the **legendary history** of the Beatles in a **non-literal way**

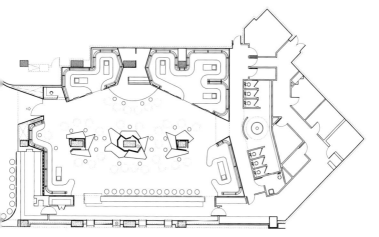

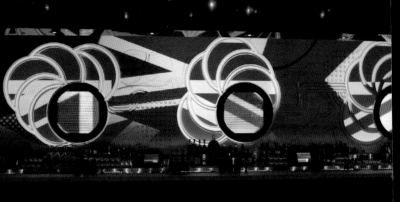
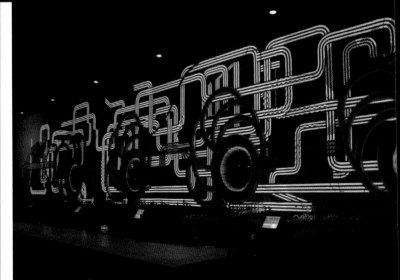

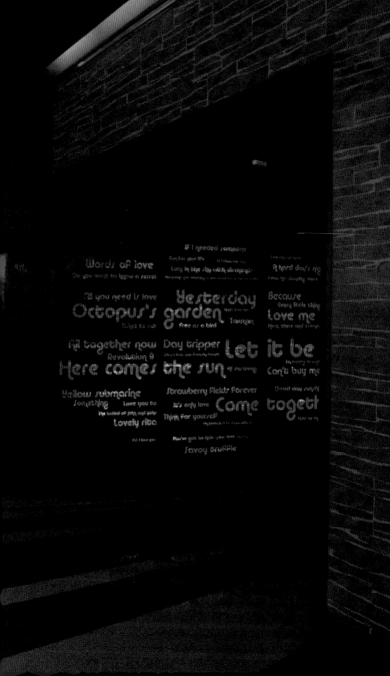

330 | **saphire bar***** | Berlin | studiolanger.com

Cream-colored leather, a zebrawood countertop and stainless steel define an elegant space

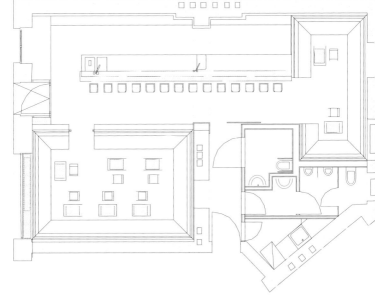

A **new kind** of experience linked to the **world of beauty,** truth and **emotio**

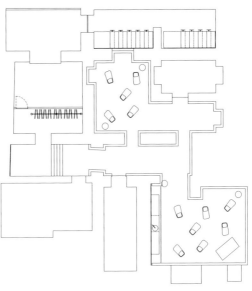

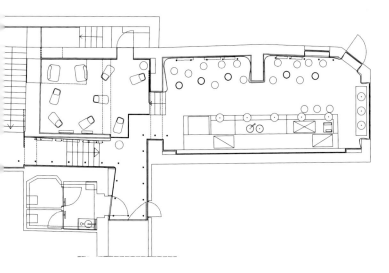

348 | **Sturecompagniet** | Stockholm | Alexander Lervik and Peter Hallén

A blend of **traditional architecture** and **modern features**

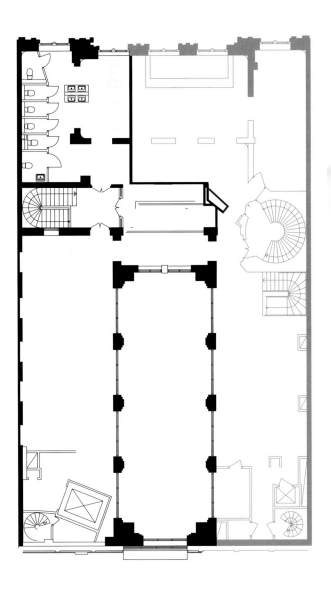

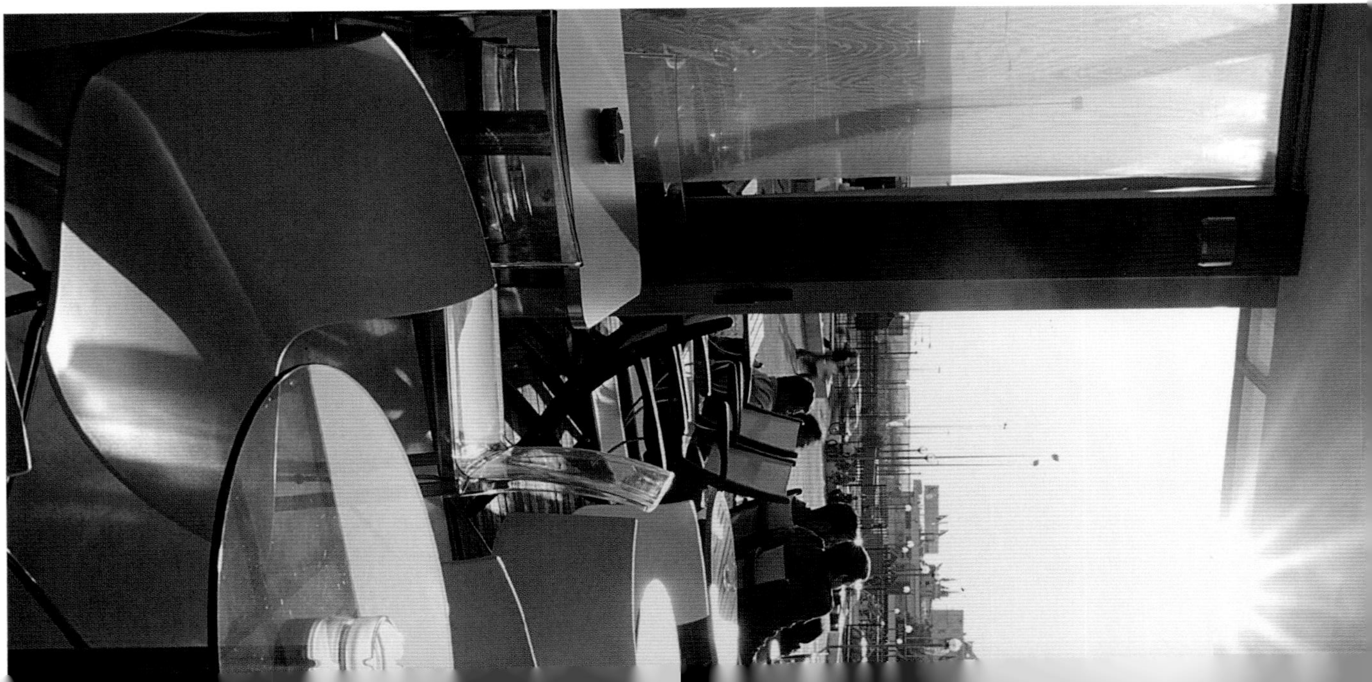

The distinctive lighting generates a live performance

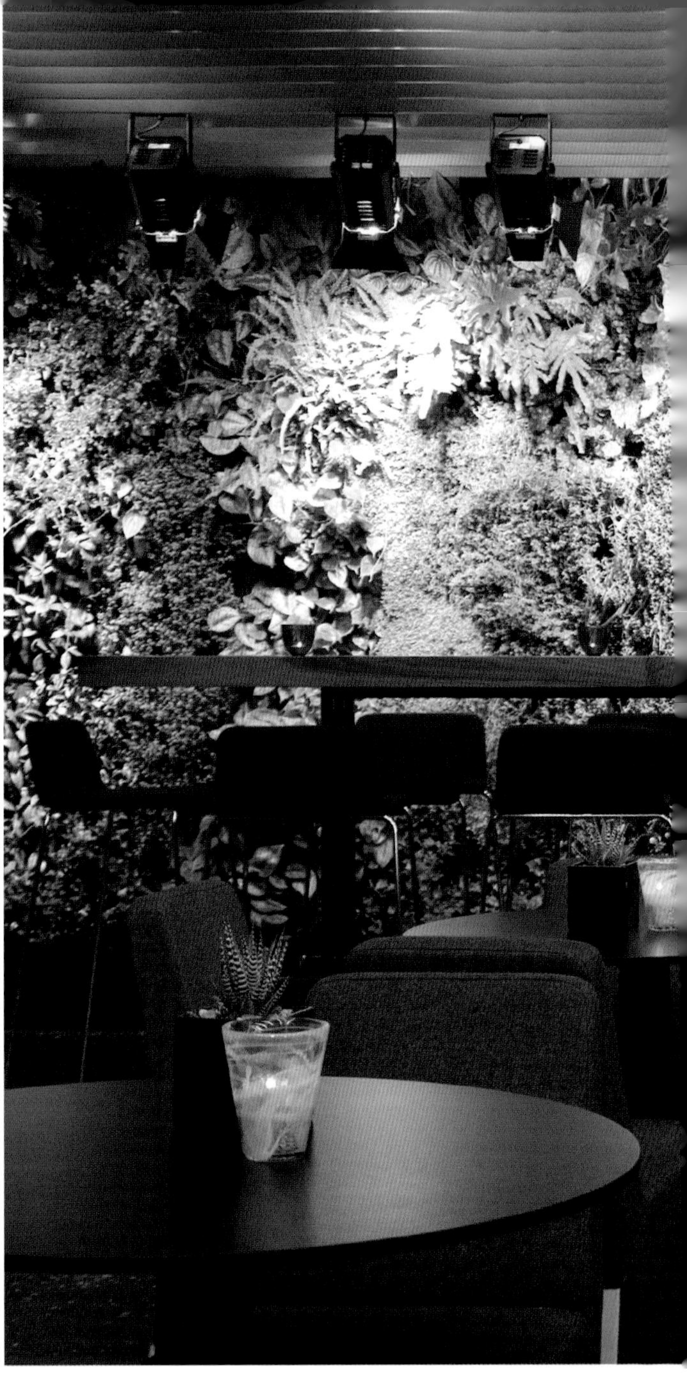

The black base of the **terrazzo floor** is customized using **green** and **yellow glass** fragments that **match the walls** and the ceiling

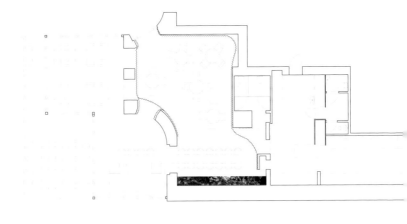

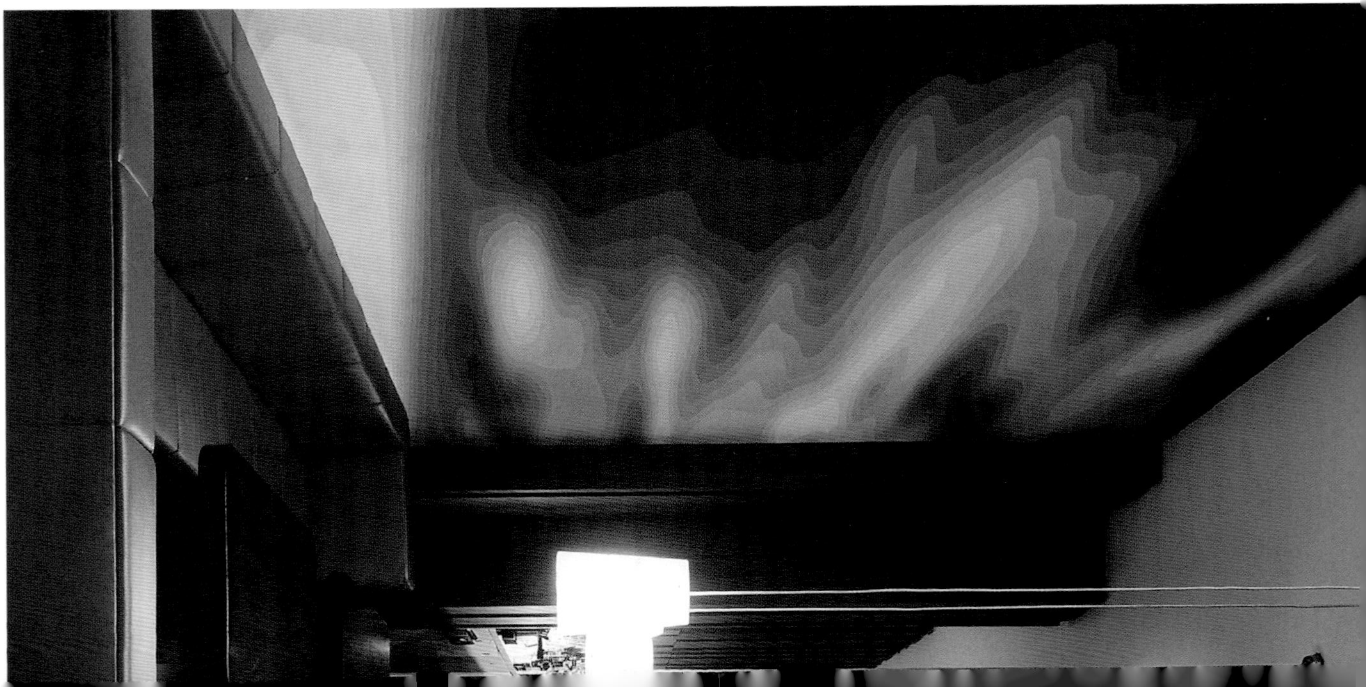

The **wooden walls** are of crossband **walnut veneer treated** in several places **with pigments** and waxes

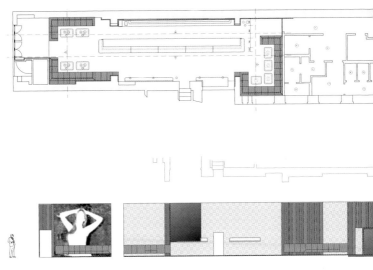

This interior **reflects** the **purity of shape** and form **over ornamental décor**

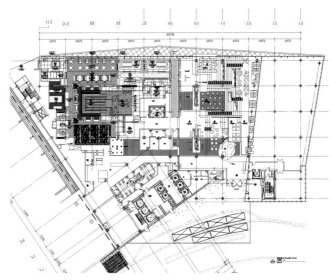

The ceiling is a **vast projectio** surface and **walls** are **planes of colored** light

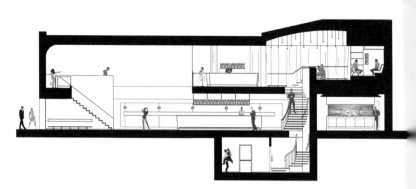

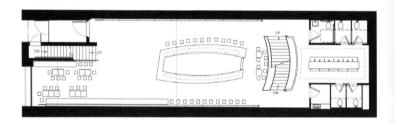

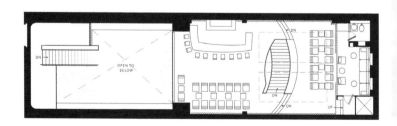

Architects Index

Picture Credits

Cover:
Revolution Lounge / Las Vegas